This
Adventure Log
Belongs To:

Chase

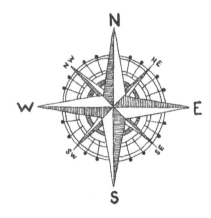

## Note to Parents:

The author in no way whatsoever assumes any responsibility
for any accidents, injuries or mishaps which may result from
any of the tools and / or ideas mentioned in this book.
Parental supervision is always advised when sharp knives
or fire is involved.

# What is an Adventure?

An adventure can be almost anything or anywhere. Seeing an experience as an adventure, is more a matter of mindset (and a little imagination) than where you actually go. It could be a family vacation, a hike, a camping trip, a visit to a local park, school field trip or just stepping out of your own back door!

# Map It:

Cartography is the art and science of making maps and can be a very useful skill to the adventurer. Maps can be very simple, or quite elaborate. If the map is of a place you visit often, making a map will help you to be more observant and to notice new things in your surroundings. If it is of a place you visit rarely or only once, your map will help you to remember your adventure there more vividly.

Your hand drawn maps can be large or small. They can be quick sketches, or contain much detail. They can be factual only, or have all the imaginary embellishments you like.

*Map making tips & ideas:*

- Use a few simple drawings to represent more. For example, a small cluster of three flowers can represent an entire patch of flowers.

- Make a "compass rose" (the "star" with letters on every map indicating direction) to show the layout of your map. This can be as simple as an arrow pointing to the North with the letter "N", or an ornate "rose" with all of the directions (North, South, East and West) noted.

- Label points of interest and paths you take on your maps. You can call them by their actual names ("Oak Tree") or give them more creative labels (such as "Fairy Village" for a cluster of mushrooms).

- To give your map a rustic, time worn look, draw it on a brown paper bag or kraft paper.

- If the location is somewhere you go often, consider hiding a "treasure" (a small tin with a note, small toy or other tiny trinket), marking the spot on your map, and giving the map to a friend.

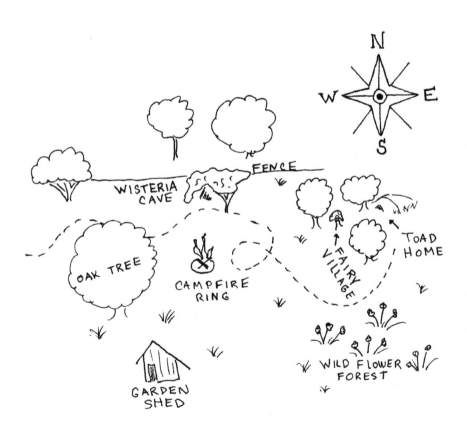

# Possible Things to Pack:

- A Compass.

- Binoculars.

- Snacks or lunch and a bottle of water.

- Bandanna or cloth handkerchief.

- Sunscreen and / or a hat.

- Pocket knife.

- Flashlight.

- Pencil and paper (and your Adventure Log).

- A small first aid kit (An empty candy tin can be reused to make a nice packable sized first aid kit.).

- Length of string or lightweight rope.

- An enamelware or stainless steel cup. A "tin cup" (and sometimes even a wooden one) has been a necessary part of an adventurer's pack for hundreds of years. Very useful for eating and drinking out of, as well as gathering small stones, acorns or berries.

# Plants to Avoid!

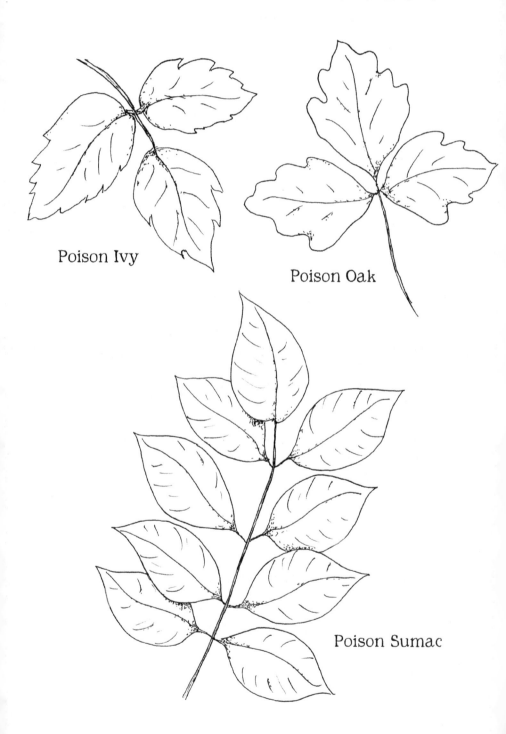

Poison Ivy

Poison Oak

Poison Sumac

# How to Use this Log:

- For each log entry write in the date and location of your adventure.

- Add in the general weather conditions. For example, sunny and hot, cold and windy, wet and muddy.

- Note any companions that were with you on the adventure. Even your dog counts!

- For the "Notes" sections, include things that you did and saw and equipment that you brought with you. Also include anything you might have learned or questions you would like to find answers to.

- In the box on second page, add in a sketch, map or printed photo. You can always re-copy your map onto larger paper later.

"Adventure is worthwhile in itself."

*Amelia Earhart*

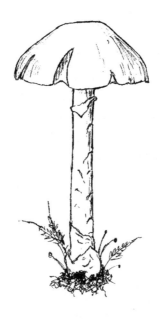

# My Ideas for Adventures:

# ← —《 Today's Adventure 》— →

Date:

Location: Pool

Weather Conditions:

Companions:

Notes:

## A Sketch, Photo or Map from this Adventure

## More Notes:

_____

_____

_____

_____

_____

_____

_____

_____

_____

_____

# Today's Adventure

Date:

Location:

Weather Conditions:

Companions:

Notes:

## A Sketch, Photo or Map from this Adventure

## More Notes:

# ←——≪ Today's Adventure ≫——→

Date:

Location:

Weather Conditions:

Companions:

Notes:

## A Sketch, Photo or Map from this Adventure

## More Notes:

_____

_____

_____

_____

_____

_____

_____

_____

_____

# Today's Adventure

Date:

Location:

Weather Conditions:

Companions:

Notes:

## A Sketch, Photo or Map from this Adventure

## More Notes:

# ←——≪ Today's Adventure ≫——→

Date:

Location:


Weather Conditions:


Companions:


Notes:

## A Sketch, Photo or Map from this Adventure

## More Notes:

# ⊲ Today's Adventure ⊳

Date:

Location:

Weather Conditions:

Companions:

Notes:

## A Sketch, Photo or Map from this Adventure

## More Notes:

# ←——≪ Today's Adventure ≫——→

Date:

Location:

Weather Conditions:

Companions:

Notes:

## A Sketch, Photo or Map from this Adventure

## More Notes:

# Today's Adventure

Date:

Location:

Weather Conditions:

Companions:

Notes:

## A Sketch, Photo or Map from this Adventure

## More Notes:

# ←——≪ Today's Adventure ≫——→

Date:

Location:


Weather Conditions:


Companions:


Notes:

## A Sketch, Photo or Map from this Adventure

## More Notes:

# ← ⊲ Today's Adventure ⊳ →

Date:

Location:

Weather Conditions:

Companions:

Notes:

## A Sketch, Photo or Map from this Adventure

## More Notes:

# ←———≪ Today's Adventure ≫———→

Date:

Location:

Weather Conditions:

Companions:

Notes:

## A Sketch, Photo or Map from this Adventure

## More Notes:

# ⟵——⊲ Today's Adventure ⊳——⟶

Date:

Location:

Weather Conditions:

Companions:

Notes:

## A Sketch, Photo or Map from this Adventure

## More Notes:
_____
_____
_____
_____
_____
_____
_____
_____
_____
_____
_____

# ←———≪ Today's Adventure ≫———→

Date:

Location:

Weather Conditions:

Companions:

Notes:

## A Sketch, Photo or Map from this Adventure

## More Notes:

# Today's Adventure

Date:

Location:

Weather Conditions:

Companions:

Notes:

## A Sketch, Photo or Map from this Adventure

## More Notes:

# ←——≪ Today's Adventure ≫——→

Date:

Location:

Weather Conditions:

Companions:

Notes:

## A Sketch, Photo or Map from this Adventure

## More Notes:

# ◁——◁ Today's Adventure ▷——▷

Date:

Location:

Weather Conditions:

Companions:

Notes:

## A Sketch, Photo or Map from this Adventure

## More Notes:

# Today's Adventure

Date:

Location:

Weather Conditions:

Companions:

Notes:

## A Sketch, Photo or Map from this Adventure

## More Notes:

_____

_____

_____

_____

_____

_____

_____

_____

_____

_____

# ◁———⊲ Today's Adventure ▷———▷

Date:

Location:

Weather Conditions:

Companions:

Notes:

## A Sketch, Photo or Map from this Adventure

## More Notes:

# ←——≪ Today's Adventure ≫——→

Date:

Location:


Weather Conditions:


Companions:


Notes:

## A Sketch, Photo or Map from this Adventure

## More Notes:

# ⇠———⫷ Today's Adventure ⫸———⇢

Date:

Location:

Weather Conditions:

Companions:

Notes:

## A Sketch, Photo or Map from this Adventure

## More Notes:

# ← —≪ Today's Adventure ≫— →

Date:

Location:

Weather Conditions:

Companions:

Notes:

## A Sketch, Photo or Map from this Adventure

## More Notes:

# ←——⟪ Today's Adventure ⟫——→

Date:

Location:


Weather Conditions:


Companions:


Notes:

## A Sketch, Photo or Map from this Adventure

## More Notes:

# ⟸——《 Today's Adventure 》——⟹

Date:

Location:

Weather Conditions:

Companions:

Notes:

## A Sketch, Photo or Map from this Adventure

## More Notes:

# Today's Adventure

Date:

Location:

Weather Conditions:

Companions:

Notes:

## A Sketch, Photo or Map from this Adventure

## More Notes:

# ←——≪ Today's Adventure ≫——→

Date:

Location:

Weather Conditions:

Companions:

Notes:

## A Sketch, Photo or Map from this Adventure

## More Notes:

# ◄────◁ Today's Adventure ▷────►

Date:

Location:

Weather Conditions:

Companions:

Notes:

## A Sketch, Photo or Map from this Adventure

## More Notes:

# ← —≪ Today's Adventure ≫— →

Date:

Location:

Weather Conditions:

Companions:

Notes:

## A Sketch, Photo or Map from this Adventure

## More Notes:

# Today's Adventure

Date:

Location:

Weather Conditions:

Companions:

Notes:

## A Sketch, Photo or Map from this Adventure

## More Notes:

# ←——≪ Today's Adventure ≫——→

Date:

Location:

Weather Conditions:

Companions:

Notes:

## A Sketch, Photo or Map from this Adventure

## More Notes:

# ◅—————◅ Today's Adventure ▻—————▻

Date:

Location:

Weather Conditions:

Companions:

Notes:

## A Sketch, Photo or Map from this Adventure

## More Notes:

# ←———≪ Today's Adventure ≫———→

Date:

Location:

Weather Conditions:

Companions:

Notes:

## A Sketch, Photo or Map from this Adventure

## More Notes:

# ◁———◁ Today's Adventure ▷———▷

Date:

Location:

Weather Conditions:

Companions:

Notes:

## A Sketch, Photo or Map from this Adventure

## More Notes:

# ←——« Today's Adventure »——→

Date:

Location:

Weather Conditions:

Companions:

Notes:

## A Sketch, Photo or Map from this Adventure

## More Notes:

# ◁———◁ Today's Adventure ▷———▷

Date:

Location:

Weather Conditions:

Companions:

Notes:

## A Sketch, Photo or Map from this Adventure

## More Notes:

# ← —« Today's Adventure »— →

Date:

Location:

Weather Conditions:

Companions:

Notes:

## A Sketch, Photo or Map from this Adventure

## More Notes:

# ⊲———⊰ Today's Adventure ⊱———⊳

Date:

Location:

Weather Conditions:

Companions:

Notes:

## A Sketch, Photo or Map from this Adventure

## More Notes:

# ←————≪ Today's Adventure ≫————→

Date:

Location:


Weather Conditions:


Companions:


Notes:

## A Sketch, Photo or Map from this Adventure

## More Notes:

_____

_____

_____

_____

_____

_____

_____

_____

_____

_____

# ◁——◁ Today's Adventure ▷——▷

Date:

Location:

Weather Conditions:

Companions:

Notes:

## A Sketch, Photo or Map from this Adventure

## More Notes:

# ←————≪ Today's Adventure ≫————→

Date:

Location:

Weather Conditions:

Companions:

Notes:

## A Sketch, Photo or Map from this Adventure

## More Notes:

# ◁——◁ Today's Adventure ▷——▷

Date:

Location:

Weather Conditions:

Companions:

Notes:

## A Sketch, Photo or Map from this Adventure

## More Notes:

# ← —≪ Today's Adventure ≫— →

Date:

Location:

Weather Conditions:

Companions:

Notes:

## A Sketch, Photo or Map from this Adventure

## More Notes:

# Today's Adventure

Date:

Location:

Weather Conditions:

Companions:

Notes:

## A Sketch, Photo or Map from this Adventure

## More Notes:

# ←——≪ Today's Adventure ≫——→

Date:

Location:

Weather Conditions:

Companions:

Notes:

## A Sketch, Photo or Map from this Adventure

## More Notes:

# ◁———⊰ Today's Adventure ⊱———▷

Date:

Location:


Weather Conditions:


Companions:


Notes:

## A Sketch, Photo or Map from this Adventure

## More Notes:

# ← —— ⋘ Today's Adventure ⋙ —— →

Date:

Location:


Weather Conditions:


Companions:


Notes:

## A Sketch, Photo or Map from this Adventure

## More Notes:

# ←———⋖ Today's Adventure ⋗———→

Date:

Location:

Weather Conditions:

Companions:

Notes:

## A Sketch, Photo or Map from this Adventure

## More Notes:

# ←——— ≪ Today's Adventure ≫ ———→

Date:

Location:

Weather Conditions:

Companions:

Notes:

## A Sketch, Photo or Map from this Adventure

## More Notes:

# ⟵——⟨ Today's Adventure ⟩——⟶

Date:

Location:


Weather Conditions:


Companions:


Notes:

## A Sketch, Photo or Map from this Adventure

## More Notes:

# ⟵——≪ Today's Adventure ≫——⟶

Date:

Location:


Weather Conditions:


Companions:


Notes:

## A Sketch, Photo or Map from this Adventure

## More Notes:

# ⟵————⟨ Today's Adventure ⟩————⟶

Date:

Location:

Weather Conditions:

Companions:

Notes:

## A Sketch, Photo or Map from this Adventure

## More Notes:

"Life is either a great adventure
or nothing."

*Helen Keller*

Made in the USA
Middletown, DE
13 May 2022

65732252R00064